Horoscope Compatibility For All The Zodiac Signs

Find Love In Your Astrology Star Sign

By
Rosemary Breen

http://psychicrevolution.com
http://compatibilityandlove.com

First Printing: 2012

ISBN: 978-1-4782-8451-2

This Book Is Dedicated To

Jill Breen

My Mum

My Inspiration

Please note: For ease of reading, parts of this document have been deliberately duplicated; for example, the description of Aries – Leo Compatibility will be found in both the Aries and the Leo sections.

Table of Contents

Books By The Author

Horoscope Compatibility
Find Love in Your Astrology Star Sign
Series

Aries
Taurus
Gemini
Cancer
Leo
Virgo
Libra
Scorpio
Sagittarius
Capricorn
Aquarius
Pisces

Horoscope Compatibility for All the Zodiac Signs

The Real Paranormal Psychic
Series

True Ghost Stories

About The Author

Rosemary Breen is an author, appreneur, internet marketer, and founder of two websites.

The first website is **PsychicRevolution.com** This site is a natural extension of Rosemary's academic research into paranormal phenomena.

The second website is **CompatibilityAndLove.com** In this website, Rosemary explores love, life and relationships from most angles, including zodiac compatibility.

Rosemary lives in Australia with her husband, two children and their Border Collie.

Twelve Star Sign Dates

Aries	March 20 - April 20
Taurus	April 21 - May 21
Gemini	May 22 - June 21
Cancer	June 22 - July 23
Leo	July 24 - August 23
Virgo	August 24 - September 23
Libra	September 24 - October 23
Scorpio	October 24 - November 22
Sagittarius	November 23 - December 21
Capricorn	December 22 - January 20
Aquarius	January 21 - February 19
Pisces	February 20 - March 19

Please Note: These dates are approximate. The exact dates do shift depending on the years that you were born. However, that shift is usually only by one day.

Introduction To Astrology

Astrology is the study of the universe and how it affects us. We don't know exactly when the study of astrology began: however, we've always been obsessed with the stars in the night sky - right back to the days of the Caveman. There is a recorded history of astrology going back over 4,000 years to the Middle East, but it is believed to be much older than that.

In the early days, only the most intelligent of scholars and officials practiced astrology; even then, it was only applied to matters of government and affairs of the country or region. In time, the information that accumulated under the umbrella of astrology became available to individuals to use in their own lives.

For the first few thousand years of its existence astrology was widely regarded as a respectable science. However, with the rise of modern science, it declined in favor only to be revived in the 1900s, when New Age spiritualism became popular.

In the early days of astrology, only five planets were known: Mercury, Venus, Mars, Jupiter, and Saturn. Today, five additional so-called planets are used, even though they aren't actually planets. These are: the Sun, Moon, Uranus, Neptune, and Pluto.

According to astrology, the Earth has always been the center of the universe. This is despite the fact that we now know that the Sun is actually at the center of our solar system.

In addition to the ten planets named above, there are twelve astrological houses.

Each planet and house has its own energy and it rules various parts of our lives and personalities. The positions of the ten planets and houses at the time a person is born make up what is called a natal chart.

Each natal chart can be described as a map of our personalities and lives. Each chart is designed to help us gain insights into ourselves. There is actually a branch of astrology called natal astrology, which looks at this particular aspect in detail.

Because there are so many different combinations of signs, planets, and houses in a natal chart, one position in a chart can be altered by another position, so no astrological position is felt 100%. When you read about your own Sun sign, you're reading about the qualities that are associated with that position, but that doesn't mean that you manifest all of them. You don't, because you have other factors in your natal chart affecting the energy of your Sun and playing a part in your personality.

Astrology is as diverse as you can be. There are different house types that can be used within a natal chart. In addition, there are other points that can be used in a natal chart, such as fixed stars and asteroids, with each ruling a different aspect of a person and their life.

There are many different forms of astrological studies. These include Vedic astrology, which is mostly used in Eastern countries, Uranian astrology, which focuses on midpoints, the exact middle between two points in a chart, and horary astrology, which casts a chart at the moment a particular question is asked, and the answer gleaned through that chart.

How astrology actually works cannot easily be answered. There are many theories of astrology that are bandied about, which are based on principles such as quantum physics, electromagnetic energy fields, even energy effects while the fetus is in the womb.

What we do know for certain is that the Moon affects humans; during a full moon, some of us even turn into "loons". This is a term derived from the word "lunar", which pertains to the Moon. Why does this happen? The way the theory goes, is that since the lunar phases are seen to affect the great oceans of the world and, humans are comprised of 70% water, the Moon somehow impacts the water within us all.

Does that seem strange? Probably, but the idea that the world was round instead of flat also seemed wacky at the time it was first suggested. Maybe in time, as modern science becomes more open to alternative views and ideas, we'll come to know much more about astrology and the solar system, and how they impact us.

In the natal chart, the three most important elements are the Sun, Moon, and ascendant - usually referred to as the triad. Why are these three the most important? The Sun, Moon, and ascendant each rule the dominant parts of our personality, and generally reflect the most about a person.

The Moon rules our emotional nature, how we react in situations, and what is needed in our lives to make us feel emotionally safe and secure. The zodiac sign, as well as the house that the Moon is in determines this aspect for each person.

The ascendant rules the outer personality - the way a person actually presents to the world. Often, people put on a mask - a public persona - when they're around others, and it is the ascendant that reflects that mask. How a person comes across in life is indicated by the sign that the ascendant falls within, as well as any planets that the person has in their first house.

When there is a planet in the first house, the person absorbs the energy of that planet into their outward personality.

An interesting point about the ascendant is that while each zodiac sign has a high vibration (positive) and low vibration (negative), people tend to only display the higher vibrations of their ascendant sign. This isn't the case with any other position. Why? Because when we present ourselves to the world, we usually want to put our best foot forward, so we naturally manifest the good parts of the sign.

The Sun rules our inner personalities - who we are to those who know us best. The ascendant could be described as the fake, sham part of the person, while the Sun is the real individual. The Sun is the person unmasked, and this is perhaps why the Sun gets the most coverage. It is the most important part of the astrological chart.

There are twelve different zodiac signs and, like the planets and the houses, each sign rules something different. As the signs progress through the zodiac wheel, they "mature", with the sign that follows, taking in the lessons learned by the previous sign.

By way of example, consider Taurus, a sign that falls in the first half of the Zodiac. Its position suggests that people born under this sign or, indeed, any of the signs in the first half of the Zodiac, still have many lessons to learn. These people tend to be lighter in energy and less astrologically mature.

It would be wrong, however, to suggest that all people born in the first half of the zodiac are immature. Rather, it is more apt to describe them as lighter. Essentially, there is usually a heaviness that comes with all the experiences endured, and the lessons learned are carried through from one zodiac sign to the next. It begins with the lightness of you, Aries, and continues through to the last sign, Pisces.

So, are you ready to learn all about you and your star sign?

Aries

March 20 – April 20

Aries, you are the first sign of the zodiac so, perhaps understandably, you are a natural born leader. You like to take the initiative in everything you do and this doesn't go unnoticed by others. You never do anything by half and in fact, you despise laziness in others. You're not a procrastinator and you prefer to get on and get things done.

Typically, you are fearless, lively, daring, energetic and a fighter. You like to explore the world but only if you can do so in your own way. People admire you for your independence and freedom of expression in all that you do. However, you tend to be headstrong and this can cause problems for you and others.

You are very focused when it comes to making your own decisions and, indeed, you are keenly aware of the role you play in creating your own destiny. Instinctively, you know what needs to be done, and you love to follow your instincts.

You have the making of a great entrepreneur but you judge your success by the goals you achieve. People who know you know that you are edgy, brisk and uncompromising and they learn to either accept this about you, or move on.

Your greatest strengths are your self-assurance and confidence. Occasionally, you come across as too assertive or self-centered. Other times, you appear strong spirited, even bold.

To be compatible with other star signs you need to control some of the more dominant traits mentioned above, plus your tendency towards possessiveness.

Aries Compatibility

Aries - Aries

This is actually a pretty good match, especially when you find the balance in your relationship. Since you are both fiery by nature, this will not necessarily be a calm partnership. Typically, Aries likes to hear loving words from their partner and if you can sort out this aspect of your relationship your partnership will work out quite well.

Aries - Taurus

Taurus is an earth sign, calm natured and rational, and these are the qualities that appeal to the Ram. In turn, the outgoing personality of the

Ram is attractive to the Bull. However, you two need to understand that this will not necessarily be an easy relationship. To help your pairing along, Aries, it would be a good idea to get approval from Taurus to socialize outside your relationship. It's likely that Taurus will oblige because the Bull likes to enjoy their 'me' time, be that alone or with friends.

Aries - Gemini

There is a single common element that you share that will either work in your favor or against you. People born under both these star signs tend to be anxious, even restless types. Sure, you both like moving on and exploring what life has to offer but do you realize how exhausting this can be? Once the exhilaration of the latest new thing starts to wane and you become restless, can you really expect your partner to just move along with you, every time? Aries, to a certain extent, you like a bit of domination in your life and the Twins can certainly give you this. On the other hand, Gemini, you need to be aware that your indirect, and at times obscure nature may drive a wedge between you and Aries. As with all relationships, communication is the key to success.

Aries - Cancer

This is a difficult relationship to start and maintain because you are both natural-born leaders. Aries don't overlook or underestimate the strong leadership qualities in your Cancer. To do so will be to your detriment. In the beginning, your Cancer partner may appear introverted but watch out, because before you know it, Aries, many of the choices you make will in fact be what Cancer wants.

Aries - Leo

There is a strong attraction between these two star signs. You both have sparkling personalities and shine with pride just for having your partner in your life. One area of your relationship that you need to watch concerns who is the dominant partner. Both of you are notorious for having dominant personalities and, if you manage to not one-up each other, this relationship should last.

Aries - Virgo

Aries, you tend to be fiery and assertive while your partner Virgo comes across as more reasonable, practical and down to earth. Strangely enough, this latter quality can get irritating for you. So, Aries, if you find your Virgo loving his work more and more, putting in longer days and not complaining about it at all, your relationship will have reached a crossroad. It is at this point that you will need to decide for yourself whether you are happy to live with this work/life imbalance or live without your Virgo.

Aries - Libra

Those born under the sign of Libra tend to very passionate and romantic and these qualities appeal to the Ram. At first, the attraction between you two may seem overwhelming but be warned, the love you share is likely to burn out almost as quickly as it started. You are opposites on the zodiac wheel and, in this instance, while you both are very attracted to each other, your relationship will only work if and when the Ram agrees to stop the chase and settle down.

Aries - Scorpio

Aries, you are generally very independent and when you attract a Scorpio you have invited someone who is intense, emotional and possessive into your life. So, how is this going to work? You are both naturally controlling by nature and your relationship will only stay the distance if and when you both manage to rein in the jealous side of your natures. This partnership can work; it just needs quite a bit of work on both your parts.

Aries - Sagittarius

People born under these two signs should get along well. You are both enthusiastic, optimistic and have positive outlooks on life. Furthermore, Aries, you are more likely than most signs to overlook your Archer's controlling ways. But have you noticed their tactlessness? Aries, while you come across as very strong willed and determined, and indeed you are these things, you need to remind Sagittarius that your strength does not make you immune to hurt. Is the Archer too critical of your appearance?

Does the Archer put down your achievements? If they do, you have a few options: toughen up, don't let Sagittarius get to you, insist that the Archer aim their insults elsewhere, or leave. Your choice! Just don't let the Archer walk over you.

Aries - Capricorn

While you respect each other's individual qualities you both have quite different approaches to life. You both love success but Aries, you prefer to skip light-heartedly through life, while your friend, the Goat, is more serious and conservative. Chances are that Aries will attempt to lighten up this relationship with Capricorn at some stage but it needs to be remembered this can only be done if the Goat agrees. You see, Capricorn is likely to dig in their heels if anyone, even their partner, tries to move them in a direction they don't want to go. Aries, if you are patient with your Capricorn, you will enjoy a remarkable relationship.

Aries - Aquarius

The Aries partner will usually take the initiative in this relationship and the Water Bearer will not keep you from doing as you please. Aries, you are adventurous and decisive, even courageous, and these qualities are much admired by your Aquarius. Be aware, however, of the issue of privacy in your relationship, as you may have different ideas about what this word means.

Aries - Pisces

Pisces is great at providing emotional support, and throwing people off track. The first quality is appealing but the latter is infuriating for an Aries. On the surface, the Pisces appears easy to dominate. This may be the case in the beginning of the relationship but, the more Aries dominates, the more the Fish will feel the need to escape. There is hope for this relationship as long as you can find a balance between domination and submission.

Taurus

April 21 – May 21

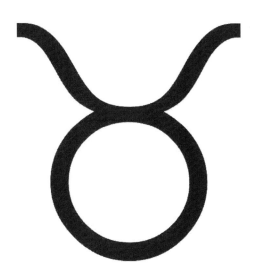

Taurus: a few words that accurately describe your personality are cautious, purposeful and practical. You are definitely not impulsive and being patient and persistent are your best qualities. Once you make up your mind to do something, rarely will you give up until it's completed. You tend to be headstrong and, to your detriment, you often have difficulty taking advice from others because of this.

You can come across as inflexible and are, oftentimes, reluctant to change your plans once your mind is made up. At the center of all this inflexibility is your dislike of change.

If anyone tries to share their wisdom or impose their knowledge on you, you're likely to let them know, in no uncertain terms, to back off. In spite of your own tendency to impose your ways on others, at heart, you would actually prefer to go with the flow. In a relationship, because of your resistance to change and your reluctance to confront conflict, you find yourself putting up with things that actually displease you, just to avoid upsetting the apple cart.

You do have a very pleasing nature, Taurus, and because of this you make good friends easily. Just be aware that your tendency towards possessiveness can come across as controlling. You may need to learn to back off a bit and give your friends and loved ones more space.

Taurus Compatibility

Taurus - Aries

Taurus is an earth sign, calm natured and rational, and these are the qualities that appeal to the Ram. In turn, the outgoing personality of the Ram is attractive to the Bull. However, you two need to understand that this will not necessarily be an easy relationship. To help your pairing along, Aries, it would be a good idea to get approval from Taurus to socialize outside your relationship. It's likely that Taurus will oblige because the Bull likes to enjoy their 'me' time, be that alone or with friends.

Taurus - Taurus

As a pair of Taureans, you understand the need for personal space and, because you both have that steady-as-she-goes approach to life, chances are the slow pace will not get to you. Not for you the big questions in life. Instead, you prefer to tend your home and nurture your relationship. A double-Taurean relationship can be a partnership for life.

Taurus - Gemini

Taurus, your Gemini partner is multi-dimensional and full of life. But, in all seriousness, is that really you, Taurus? The nature of the Bull tends to be more staid, almost prone to inertia compared to the capricious, fun-loving approach to life that characterizes the Twins. You two may enjoy each other, for a while at least, but be wary of trying to form any long-lasting relationship with each other. You probably don't have enough in common to sustain anything more than a fleeting partnership.

Taurus - Cancer

Those born under these two signs tend to be homebodies and very affectionate. Sounds ideal, doesn't it? It is, until you realize that there will be an ongoing tug-of-war between the two of you as to who will be the main giver of affection and who will be the primary receiver. You are both nurturing and loyal and, when it comes time to commit to each other, you both prefer to take your time and get it right. However, once you are committed, chances are you will plan everything together – your careers, your finances, your home; in fact, you will probably map out your whole lives together. Enjoy!

Taurus - Leo

There is a strong attraction between these two star signs. You both have sparkling personalities and shine with pride just for having your partner in your life. One area of your relationship that you need to watch concerns who is the dominant partner. Both of you are notorious for having dominant personalities and, if you manage to not one-up each other, this relationship should last.

Taurus - Virgo

You are both earth signs and practical by nature. However, this doesn't mean that you are entirely compatible. Sure, you are great lovers but there is more to life than the bedroom, wouldn't you agree? Virgo, you tend to take being practical and organized way too far for you Taurean partner, and your tendency to over-organize may ultimately be the downfall of your relationship with your Bull.

Taurus - Libra

Libra, you are quite the romantic and your passionate nature is very attractive to the practical Bull. The Libran gives 100% to each and every relationship they have and this approach suits the hedonistic, sensual Taurus. Libra, remember your symbol is the Scales and, when it comes to matters of the heart, you need to be aware that you can be easily thrown off balance. So, take care and don't run off at the first chance with someone new, leaving your Bull wondering what went wrong. While it may be in your nature to do so, it is up to you whether you choose to or not.

Taurus - Scorpio

Can the Bull withstand the sting of the Scorpion? If anyone can, yes, a Taurean can. By nature, Scorpio is dominating, even possessive, and while at first the Bull is able to withstand the sheer intensity of the Scorpion's focus, eventually they will be worn down by it and leave the relationship. That is not necessarily a bad thing for Taurus because the Bull does like its own company. So, Scorpio, do you feel confident enough in yourself and your relationship with your Bull to let them have their personal space? If you don't, you will lose them.

Taurus - Sagittarius

The key word to this relationship is faithfulness. Taurus, do you fully understand that when Sagittarius pledges their undying love and devotion to you they really do mean it – in their own way? Throughout their lives, Sagittarians tend to attract a lot of partners and this long relationship record has a tendency to upset the much more faithful Taurus. So, at the first sign that Sagittarius is back playing the love field, Taurus, you would be well advised to take your leave and move on.

Taurus - Capricorn

Taurus and Capricorn are both practical types of people, and devoted lovers. However, the tenderness that you share in your relationship will depart, even if the Goat doesn't, if Capricorn feels taken for granted in any way. So, if there's the possibility that either of you is not looking for a long-term, monogamous relationship, then you will both be better off looking elsewhere for what you need. You are both earth signs but that bond is not enough to necessarily bind you together indefinitely.

Taurus - Aquarius

This is a match that can go either way. Ask yourselves this! Is there something about the other that seems to inexplicably draw you to them, even though on the surface you are so different? You probably realize by now that your relationship requires an enormous amount of work, compromise, and understanding. That's a big ask for anyone! However, given the innate determination that you both share, you may just be able to add this relationship to your personal lists of achievements.

Taurus - Pisces

Pisces, you are everyone's soul mate, or so it seems – even the Bull's. Give each other space and 'me' time and you will get along well. Taurus, you are known for your perseverance and this personal quality is enough to at least get Pisces' attention. Taurus, you will keep the interest of your Pisces partner if you are prepared to receive all that the bountiful and nurturing Pisces has to give.

Gemini

May 22 – June 21

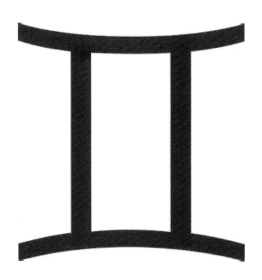

Among your many qualities, Gemini, are your good communication skills and your innate intelligence. You are also known for your ability to express yourself and your critical thinking skills. Often these personal qualities leave you wondering why you don't see things the ways others do. However, when you come across someone who is quick witted and a good conversationalist, with a natural ability to discuss things in a deep and meaningful way, you are immediately attracted to them.

You have a wide array of interests and, in fact, you take great pride in challenging yourself to achieve things that are outside your comfort zone. You are attracted to activities that challenge you and you often reign supreme in those sports that require you to draw upon your ability to strategize and use your brainpower.

Gemini, do you realize that taking some acting lessons would actually be good for you? It's not so much the acting part of the lessons that will be good for you. More, it is the opportunity to express yourself, stretch yourself and socialize all at the same time that could appeal to you.

People love to be around a Gemini. You are adaptable, comfortable when getting to know others and, as a relaxed, intelligent communicator, you are great at putting others at ease.

You, Gemini, have the potential to pair up with a number of zodiac signs. So, enjoy the array of choices before you – you probably are doing this already.

Gemini Compatibility

Gemini - Aries

There is a single common element that you share that can either work in your favor or against you. People born under both of these star signs tend to be anxious, even restless. Sure, you both love moving on and exploring what life has to offer but do you realize how exhausting this can be? Once the exhilaration of the latest new thing starts to wane and you become restless, can you really expect your partner to just move along with you, every time? Aries, to a certain extent, you like a bit of domination in your life and the Twins can certainly give you this. On the other hand, Gemini, you need to be aware that your indirect, and at times obscure nature may drive a wedge between you and Aries. As with all relationships, communication is the key to success.

Gemini - Taurus

Taurus, your Gemini partner is multi-dimensional and full of life. But, in all seriousness, is that really you, Taurus? The nature of the Bull tends to be more staid, almost prone to inertia compared to the capricious, fun-loving approach to life that characterizes the Twins. You two may enjoy each other, for a while at least, but be wary of trying to form any long-lasting relationship with each other. You probably don't have enough in common to sustain anything more than a fleeting partnership.

Gemini - Gemini

Gemini, you and your mate, the other Gemini, do get on well but for how long will your relationship last? Does this really matter to you anyway? Why not enjoy each other – you know each other so well – and not worry about where this relationship will take you? There is certainly a lack of groundedness in the Gemini-Gemini connection but, between you, you two have a lot in common, including a love of movement and activity. Explore the world as fully as you can with your partner and, if the relationship ends, at least you will both have wonderful memories.

Gemini - Cancer

A person born under the sign of Cancer tends to be maternal or paternal. So, how does this quality match up with the fickle Gemini? Essentially, you are opposites and, while this match is unlikely to be long lasting, you do have some complementary characteristics that will make your relationship interesting. Gemini, do you love to go on dates? Are you even a serial dater perhaps? Cancer, do you believe more in dating for mating? Are you in the market to find your soul mate? Cancer, do you believe in nurturing and savoring a long-term relationship? Can you both see where your fundamental difference lies? It is this very issue that could even prevent you from getting your relationship off the ground in the first place.

Gemini - Leo

These two star signs are compatible. You both like adventure and being out and about and doing things. So, chances are, you will enjoy a lifetime of activity together. Gemini, your Lion absolutely loves all the attention you bestow on them – the more attentive you are, the more Leo falls under your spell. But wait, Leo, have you noticed how equally attentive

15

Gemini is to everyone they like? So, is the Lion/Twins relationship the real thing or just a shadow of a true relationship? That depends! If you are both looking for loads of energy, fun, and sociability in your relationship then you are made for each other. If you are looking for more, or different from this, you will have to decide for yourself.

Gemini - Virgo

People born under these two star signs tend to be wonderful communicators. You love to express your feelings, ask loads of questions, gather information, and check and recheck the details with your partner. The differences between you lie in the way you approach the whole communication thing. Gemini, you're quite capable of adequately scanning multiple sources of information at the same time while your partner, Virgo, tends to focus on one source at a time. Just notice, which of you is likely to be reading the paper, flicking through the TV channels and chatting away quite happily while the other is drilling down into the contents of one magazine only, determined to fully understand the topic under consideration. You do complement each other but Gemini, you will have to go beyond skimming if you want Virgo to stay around.

Gemini - Libra

This is a good match. You are both air signs and should be highly compatible. Both of you enjoy intellectual pursuits and, together, you should also enjoy a good social life. However, your styles of socializing and partying are quite different and your approaches may cause some friction between you. Libra, at parties you tend to hold back and attract people who interest you. On the other hand, your partner, Gemini, will happily cruise off into the middle of the crowd and start chatting away. A word of advice! Gemini, try and slow down a bit and listen to your Libran partner and you will have a match that lasts as long as you both want.

Gemini - Scorpio

What an unusual pairing. It's as though you two are from different planets. Have you ever really got to know anyone like your partner before? The essence of who and what you are is so truly foreign to each of you.

Therein lies the mystery, the intrigue, the allure and the attraction. Add to this, the sociability of Gemini and the passionate nature of Scorpio and this becomes an intriguing mix. Will your relationship last? Stranger things have happened than will come out of this pairing but you may be wise to enjoy each other in the moment and take each day as it comes.

Gemini - Sagittarius

You are both free spirits. You dislike being pinned down too much, are happiest when exploring life and you both welcome change and challenges. You are also both risk takers and so one or both of you needs to be more careful than your nature would suggest. Unfortunately, there are not the usual checks and balances that usually arise in relationships and so you are likely to push the limits too far in life, in your relationship and in all that you do together. Be aware of this to avoid unnecessary suffering. The Archer likes things straight up – no waffle, no frills, no embellishments – so Gemini, get to the point as soon and as often as you can when talking to your partner. Save your sweet lead-ins for others. Conversely, the Archer would do well to curb their bluntness and soften their words when speaking to the Twins.

Gemini - Capricorn

These star signs are opposites. Gemini, you are the outgoing member of this partnership. You love people and socializing and being involved and, Capricorn, you are far more reserved than your partner. So, the question for you is this: can you both accept your obvious differences and not be tempted to change each other too much? If you can, there will be longevity in your relationship. If you can't resist the temptation to change your partner your relationship will be short lived.

Gemini - Aquarius

You are both air signs and that's a good thing. Both of you love freedom and are happy not weaving a web to entrap your partner. This, too, is a good sign. So, where is the catch? Have you noticed the lack of depth in your relationship yet? The Water Bearer loves tackling a cause – ecology, the environment, education, equality – and Aquarius, while your partner may start off as enthusiastically as you do, ultimately Gemini is likely to lose focus. Knowing this fundamental difference gives you a chance to adjust your expectations of your relationship. You can make a good go of this and, romantically, you are very compatible.

Gemini - Pisces

These two star signs are generally up for trying anything new and, within this pairing, there is much to explore. Both Pisces and Gemini enjoy their own personal freedom and, indeed, are happy to accommodate this quality in their partnership. Gemini, while you are attracted to Pisces' sensitivity and wisdom, to ensure your relationship lasts, you need to hone your intuition a bit more, so that you can develop a deeper understanding of your Piscean partner.

Cancer

June 22 – July 23

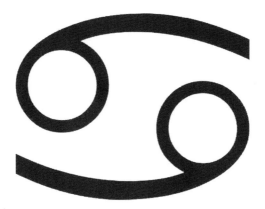

Cancer is a water sign and those born under the sign of the Crab are very spiritual. Cancerians can also be regarded as the most nurturing of all the signs of the Zodiac. This is both good news – who doesn't love being nurtured? – and bad news. There is a big difference between nurturing and smothering and some people born under the sign of Cancer don't know where the line is between the two. The point is – don't overdo the nurturing, Cancer.

As a Cancerian, you tend to be very emotional, sentimental, more intuitive than most, as well as caring and compassionate. Your sensitivity attracts others to you and they, in turn, get not only your shoulder to cry on but also excellent advice from you. People tend to rely on you heavily, Cancer, not only for the words of encouragement and support that you offer but also for your ability to reduce the stress in their lives.

Ideally, the best occupations for you are those in which you help others. This seems to be what you do best, and what you enjoy most. You naturally pick up on other people's moods and energies and, while this can be helpful, you need to be careful not to overload yourself with other people's baggage.

You are prone to mood swings and, in part, this is due to the influence of the waxing and waning of the moon. You may find you have moments when your emotions see you soar to extreme highs, and the next moment you find yourself plunging to the depths of despair. Try and iron out some of these highs and lows, Cancer – for your sake and the sake of those you love.

Relationship-wise, you will find that you are attracted to and are more compatible with those who are nurturing, just like you.

Cancer Compatibility

Cancer - Aries

This is a difficult relationship to start and maintain because you are both natural born leaders. Aries don't overlook or underestimate the strong leadership qualities in your Cancer. To do so will be to your detriment. In the beginning, your Cancer partner may appear introverted but watch out, because before you know it, Aries, many of the choices you make will in fact be what Cancer wants.

Cancer - Taurus

Those born under these two signs tend to be homebodies and very affectionate. Sounds ideal, doesn't it? It is, until you realize that there will be an ongoing tug-of-war between the two of you as to who will be the main giver of affection and who will be the primary receiver. You are both nurturing and loyal and, when it comes time to commit to each other, you both prefer to take your time and get it right. However, once you are committed, chances are you will plan everything together – your careers, your finances, your home; in fact, you will probably map out your whole lives together. Enjoy!

Cancer - Gemini

A person born under the sign of Cancer tends to be maternal or paternal. So, how does this quality match up with the fickle Gemini? Essentially, you are opposites and, while this match is unlikely to be long lasting, you do have some complementary characteristics that will make your relationship interesting. Gemini, do you love to go on dates? Are you even a serial dater perhaps? Cancer, do you believe more in dating for mating? Are you in the market to find your soul mate? Cancer, do you believe in nurturing and savoring a long-term relationship? Can you both see where your fundamental difference lies? It is this very issue that could even prevent you from getting your relationship off the ground in the first place.

Cancer - Cancer

On the one hand, a relationship with someone of the same star sign can work out because you are similar. On the other hand, however, there is always a good chance that you will both be fighting for the same ground. Cancer, you are a very nurturing sign and when there are two of you involved, you will either overwhelm each other with kindness and love or wear yourselves out with all your mood swings. Yes, Cancer, you are prone to many highs and lows and your reluctance to share your deepest, most inner feelings with your partner will probably mean there is little room for either of you to grow in this relationship. The solution: try and build some 'me' time into your relationship and it may last longer.

Cancer - Leo

Are you familiar with the term co-dependent? If you are in this relationship it may be wise for you both to brush up on the definition and treatment of this condition. While you are both caring by nature, things can and do go wrong when the relationship becomes unbalanced. Leo, if you are not utterly adored, even worshipped, you can turn on your partner. So, Cancer, putting this bluntly, are you prepared to fawn over your Lion indefinitely, ad finitum, ad nauseum (and every other Latin term that springs to mind)? If you are, bravo! Your devotion of Leo will keep your Lion right by your side. Leo, for your part, to keep Cancer happy you need to schedule regular 'at home' time because, at heart, Cancer is a true homebody. If you two can move to accommodate each other in these ways you should enjoy your relationship.

Cancer - Virgo

You two are a good match for each other. You are both helpful and caring and your relationship is destined to thrive. You both love planning, so plan together. Are you both inclined to be stay-at-homes? If you are, then be careful that your relationship does not become too stifling. Intensity is one thing; being suffocated is another. Furthermore, you both have the tendency to be overbearing and controlling and need to guard against this. Having said all this, however, this is a good relationship and one that should work well for you both.

Cancer - Libra

Libra, you are a romantic and your charms will seduce your Cancer, at least in the beginning. The Crab has a very nurturing nature and so, when you two meet, you will probably both feel like you have met your twin. It's almost as though you've finally found someone who understands the real you. Cancer, you need to relax and enjoy your relationship with Libra. Sure, this partnership may seem too good to be true but it doesn't have to be so. Together, you can live the dream.

Cancer - Scorpio

Scorpio has a tendency to be jealous. Can you deal with this side of your partner, Cancer? Or is it too much like looking into the mirror? It could very well feel like this because you are both familiar with the ugly side of jealousy. Sure, there are differences in where your jealousy springs from – for one it is ego driven and, for the other, oftentimes your jealousy stems from your own personal insecurity. There is a trick to avoiding claws and fangs and clashing of heads and that is to mark out your own territory, within your relationship. You are compatible. You just need to learn how to live together.

Cancer - Sagittarius

Upfront, answer this question. Both of you! Why do you want to be together? Have you given much thought to what each of you brings to your relationship? Individually, both your star signs are great. However, when you two get together is when the clashes seem to start. Have you noticed that about your relationship yet? If you want to, and if it's not too late, why don't you consider ending this relationship and waiting for more suitable partners? If you are already committed to each other then, Cancer, you might like to try backing off and giving your Sagittarius space – loads of space. As you may have gathered by now, (or perhaps you haven't worked it out yet), your Centaur does not like to be hemmed in. And, Cancer, what can you do to help your relationship? Try curbing your need to smother your partner – truth be told, they don't like feeling stifled. These are big asks of both of you.

Cancer - Capricorn

You are both deeply attracted to each other and share a mutual love of stability. This is a great start for your relationship. However, because you are both very predictable, even conservative, things may get a bit boring even for you. To avoid this, all that really needs to happen is for the Goat to open up more and share their feelings with their partner. Get the communication right, avoid the rut and you two could be on the road to a lasting relationship – one that is based on friendship, companionship, loyalty and balance.

Cancer - Aquarius

Cancer, you and your Aquarian partner are both friendly and intense. Aquarius, you would do well to learn to be more compassionate with your Crab. Cancer, try not to run, at least in the beginning, from the conservative lifestyle that you two will no doubt build together. If you do feel the need to flee, chances are you will ruin your relationship because you will likely find comfort and excitement in the arms of another. It is unlikely this relationship will last a lifetime but you may as well enjoy each other for a while at least.

Cancer - Pisces

Cancer, you and Pisces are similar natured. You both tend to be emotional and are sympathetic and compassionate. However, for this relationship to last, you both need to let down your guards. The Fish will embrace the Crab. In return, the Crab needs to be wary of not overwhelming the Fish. If you both really work at your relationship it will work but, if either of you is unwilling to really compromise, it is probably best that you move on. Cancer, you hate lying and Pisces, while you are not prone to outright lying, your exaggerations will get to your Crab partner. If both of you are willing to work at this partnership it will happen, if only

Leo

July 24 – August 23

Leo, your star sign shines brightly. You are dazzling, flamboyant, irresistible, self-motivated and dynamic. An all-round extrovert! No wonder people enjoy having you near. You leave your mark on everything you do - your work, your social life, even your love life. Nothing gets in the way of your ambitions and your fighting spirit.

You are generous by nature and you are disappointed when others don't match your big-heartedness. In fact, it's your determination to succeed and your giant personality that define who you are and who you enjoy being with.

Seemingly, always at the height of your game, you attract people towards you with your energy and vibrancy and, in return, you expect nothing from them. Just having those you love and care about close to you seems to be enough reward for you.

Sometimes the strong sense of self that you consistently exude can be misinterpreted. For this reason, you may have to consciously tone down your personality and your ways. In this way you will avoid coming across as too much of a show-off.

Typically, you have lots of energy and enjoy being involved with things that are meaningful or social activities that are adventurous and allow you to expend some of your excess energy. As a natural-born leader, people are drawn to you and typically they look to you for guidance.

A relationship with the Lion will always be fresh.

Leo Compatibility

Leo - Aries

There is a strong attraction between these two star signs. You both have sparkling personalities and shine with pride just for having your partner in your life. One area of your relationship that you need to watch concerns who is the dominant partner. Both of you are notorious for having dominant personalities and, if you manage to not one-up each other, this relationship should last.

Leo - Taurus

On the surface, this star sign combination does not look great. However, there is much to be hopeful about here. Leo, not only are you outgoing and confident, you are also generous and warm and Taurus finds these qualities very alluring. Taurus, ask yourself this, do you adore your Lion? Can you commit to Leo completely? If you can, then there's a very good chance that you two will go far together.

Leo - Gemini

These two star signs are compatible. You both like adventure and being out and about and doing things. So, chances are, you will enjoy a lifetime of activity together. Gemini, your Lion absolutely loves all the attention you bestow on them – the more attentive you are, the more Leo falls under your spell. But wait, Leo, have you noticed how equally attentive Gemini is to everyone they like? So, is the Lion/Twins relationship the real thing or just a shadow of a true relationship? That depends! If you are both looking for loads of energy, fun, and sociability in your relationship then you are made for each other. If you are looking for more, or different from this, you will have to decide for yourself.

Leo - Cancer

Are you familiar with the term co-dependent? If you are in this relationship it may be wise for you both to brush up on the definition and treatment of this condition. While you are both caring by nature, things can and do go wrong when the relationship becomes unbalanced. Leo, if you are not utterly adored, even worshipped, you can turn on your partner. So, Cancer, putting this bluntly, are you prepared to fawn over your Lion indefinitely, ad finitum, ad nauseum (and every other Latin term that springs to mind)? If you are, bravo! Your devotion of Leo will keep your Lion right by your side. Leo, for your part, to keep Cancer happy you need to schedule regular 'at home' time because, at heart, Cancer is a true homebody. If you two can move to accommodate each other in these ways you should enjoy your relationship.

Leo - Leo

Leo is an energetic sign and so, in this double relationship, you can expect a doubling of most things. You will spend twice as long sizing each other up; there will be double the effort expended in assessing each other; you will think twice as long about who will wield the most power in your relationship; and there will be double the competition between yourselves. Do you get the idea? This will be a full-on relationship. So, keep your pride in check at all times and early on in your pairing sort out who will play the role of the king and who will play the role of associate. Then, if you can stick to your roles, there's a good chance that your relationship will stay the distance.

Leo - Virgo

You both love glitz and glam and shiny baubles. Have you noticed you have this in common yet? Of course, there is much more to a Virgo than glitter and trinkets but, initially at least, this is the quality that will attract and hold the Lion. What will sustain your relationship? Hard work! Fortunately Virgo, you are a good worker, especially when it comes to relationships. Leo, you are very loyal – another admirable quality and one that will help keep the two of you together. Is there any more to this relationship than what people see on the surface? There may not be. Take a look beyond the abovementioned qualities and ask yourselves, what do you actually have in common? Are your responses enough for you? Only you know the answer to that.

Leo - Libra

Libra, you are a social animal and this is a very attractive quality to your Lion. While you both enjoy climbing the social ladder neither of you is crass enough to mention it outright. Your romantic relationship may start out as a friendship and, if so, this will form the cornerstone of your ongoing partnership. You are highly compatible. You are both romantics; you are both keen and willing to open up fully to your partner. Together, Leo and Libra could build a relationship that lasts a lifetime.

Leo - Scorpio

A common and strong link between you two is your determination. Chances are, in the beginning of your relationship, you will both show off your passionate sides. Later on, however, this burning passion you both feel could turn into hot clashes; that is, unless Scorpio agrees to be the power behind Leo's throne. Your relationship is ruled by domination and this is not necessarily an easy route for either of you to travel. Try being kinder to each other. Be gentle on yourselves and your relationship. That way, you may enjoy your partnership, rather than just endure it.

Leo - Sagittarius

What a happy couple this star sign combination makes! Your sunny dispositions and love of life and fun shine through for all the world to see. One sticking point in your relationship could be the matter of freedom. Leo, have you noticed how you love to reign in your Sagittarius? This is not a particularly good thing to do if you want the Archer to stick around. Sagittarius, you love your freedom and, there is no doubt about it, your Lion must allow you to roam freely. How else can it be? Leo, you are a very sensitive star sign and, if Sagittarius hurts you with their barbed comments you will quickly retreat from them to lick your wounds. Be aware of this, Sagittarius, and don't purposely set out to hurt your Lion's pride. You may just hurt Leo once too often.

Leo - Capricorn

Capricorn, you are more reserved and less open to expressing your feelings than your partner, Leo. This difference will probably be the primary source of discord in your relationship. You two are certainly good where business matters are concerned but when it comes to the romantic side of your relationship, you will have to work extra hard to make it work. Capricorn, you need to learn to be more open with your feelings and show affection for your Lion in public more. Similarly, the Lion partner needs to allow the Goat to get on with their work. You are both intrinsically loyal and, if you find a good balance, your relationship will flourish. Look for that compromise position and you will enjoy a happy relationship.

Leo - Aquarius

Mmm! This is a bit of a strange coupling. Aquarius, you need to try and be more personable when Leo is around. Otherwise, you'll find that you've kept the personal entourage of friends that surrounds you and you will have lost Leo. The Water Bearer likes freedom so don't try and cramp their style. At heart, Aquarians are freedom-loving creatures who strongly resist any attempts to hem them in. So, Leo, even though you love to rule, if you impose your authority over Aquarius, they will simply turn and leave you.

Leo - Pisces

Pisces is usually out to shower the one they love with love and loads of affection and attention. This suits Leo just fine. To an outsider, this relationship looks like one in which the Lion rules and the Fish is happy to be submissive. However, things are not always what they seem when Pisces is involved. Pisces, you are more secretive than your Lion partner and Leo, you love to put all of you out there on display for others to see and admire. For this relationship to last you will have to indulge and accommodate the marked difference you have. Are you up to the challenge?

Virgo

August 24 – September 23

You, Virgo, are a perfectionist. You like things to be clean, organized and tidy and you are meticulous when it comes to getting things done. Your attention to detail is very obvious to others who may even refer to you as anal. So try and not overdo this perfection thing. It can be off-putting to potential partners.

Virgo, you tend to be critical of the world around you and you have extremely high standards not only for yourself but for all the people in your life. Beware: some people resent this. Your standards tend to be too high, unrealistic, even unattainable. Yes, we know that you, as a Virgo, are self-critical and, although it may not be obvious to all, you don't expect anything of anyone else that you wouldn't expect from yourself. But, that's not the point. Virgo, you need to realize that it's not your place to set goals for others and to expect them to march to your own tune, especially if you are in a relationship with them.

You do openly express criticism but this is typically after you've reflected long and hard on the situation. Some people love this about you – your considered approach. They're also attracted to your natural insight and value your advice and knowledge, often turning to you for help in times of need.

Virgo, your tendency is to be stable, grounded, and practical and you are even able to relax when you're in a stable relationship with someone who makes you feel secure. Try to not over-analyze your relationships, especially at the outset, or they might not even get off the ground.

Virgo Compatibility

Virgo - Aries

Aries, you tend to be fiery and assertive while your partner, Virgo, comes across as more reasonable, practical and down-to-earth. Strangely enough, this latter quality can get irritating for you. So, Aries, if you find your Virgo loving his work more and more, putting in longer days and not complaining about it at all, your relationship will have reached a crossroad. It is at this point that you will need to decide for yourself whether you are happy to live with this work/life imbalance or live without your Virgo.

Virgo - Taurus

You are both earth signs and practical by nature. However, this doesn't mean that you are entirely compatible. Sure you are great lovers but there is more to life than the bedroom, wouldn't you agree? Virgo, you tend to take being practical and organized way too far for your Taurean partner and your tendency to over-organize may ultimately be the downfall of your relationship with your Bull.

Virgo - Gemini

People born under these two star signs tend to be wonderful communicators. You love to express your feelings, ask loads of questions, gather information, and check and recheck the details with your partner. The differences between you lie in the way you approach the whole communication thing. Gemini, you're quite capable of adequately scanning multiple sources of information at the same time while your partner, Virgo, tends to focus on one source at a time. Just notice, which of you is likely to be reading the paper, flicking through the TV channels and chatting away quite happily while the other is drilling down into the contents of one magazine only, determined to fully understand the topic under consideration. You do complement each other but Gemini, you will have to go beyond skimming if you want Virgo to stay around.

Virgo - Cancer

You two are a good match for each other. You are both helpful and caring and your relationship is destined to thrive. You both love planning, so plan together. Are you both inclined to be stay-at-homes? If you are, then be careful that your relationship does not become too stifling. Intensity is one thing; being suffocated is another. Furthermore, you both have the tendency to be overbearing and controlling and need to guard against this. Having said all this, however, this is a good relationship and one that should work well for you both.

Virgo - Leo

You both love glitter and shine. Have you noticed that yet? Of course, there is more to a Virgo than glitz and glamour but, initially at least, this quality will attract and hold the Lion. However, what will keep you together is hard work and Virgo, you are a good worker, especially when it comes to relationships. Leo, you are very loyal – another admirable quality that will help hold the two of you together. But is there any more to this partnership? There may not be. So, look beyond the above qualities and ask yourselves, what do we have in common?

Virgo - Virgo

Virgo plus Virgo means double the help. Characteristically, Virgo loves to give a helping hand and when you two get together, you can hardly give enough to the other. You both love talking and communicating and have little difficulty in asking for what you want from the other. So, where's the catch? You are both accustomed to being the leader, the one with the plan, the person who always has the situation under control. So, you can't both be in this role all the time. Take turns at supporting each other and, rather than trying to help each other 24/7, look beyond your relationship and find a cause that really needs your help. That outward turning will be the making of you both individually and collectively.

Virgo - Libra

Upfront, let's be honest. Being born under the sign of Virgo can mean being born with the potential to be tactless. So, in your relationship with Libra, guess who is likely to be the critical one? Guess who calls a spade a spade? Virgo, your frankness is too much for your more sensitive partner, Libra. So, if this relationship is to last, you need to take care what you say to Libra and how you say it. Libra, you are outwardly romantic and love little gestures of affection. Unfortunately, your partner will not be familiar with this way of expressing love and, if you want these romantic signs of affection, you're going to have to teach Virgo. Typically, the Virgin prefers to show their affection by doing things for you, rather than telling you. Can you live with this, Libra? Alternatively, can you learn a new way of expressing love, Virgo?

Virgo - Scorpio

People born under these signs tend to be very practical and this can get very annoying. Virgo, do you nag your Scorpion? You don't need to, you know. They know what's expected of them but the Virgin just can't help themselves. Try and relax around each other more. You are a good match. When you, Scorpio, become quiet, it could mean you're going into one of your moods. It could also mean you want time to yourself. Virgo, learn to read your partner's moods and respect their need for solitude. There is always plenty for you to do to keep yourself busy.

Virgo - Sagittarius

Sagittarius, you like experimenting with different relationships and in Virgo you will find an interesting partner. That is, if you get the chance to partner with the Virgin. You see, Virgo is far more choosey than you are. They will let you know in no uncertain terms what they think about your long list of relationships, your seemingly tarty behavior, and your obvious need to explore different couplings. Your style is not Virgo's style! So, Virgo, while you may feel that the excitement you bring to your relationship with the Centaur is a valuable contribution don't be surprised if you are left feeling underappreciated in this partnership.

Virgo - Capricorn

You are both practical earth signs and while this down-to-earth quality might seem boring to some, to you it is the stuff of which your love is made. You are very compatible. Yours is a match made in the stars. So, enjoy each other and don't worry what the outside world may think of you and your mutual love of financial planning, etc. You are a good match for each other.

Virgo - Aquarius

The bond between Virgo and Aquarius is more intellectual than emotional. This is an unusual coupling, to say the least. For your relationship to have a chance of success, the Virgin need to lighten up and the Water Bearer needs to resist the temptation to rebel, just because they can. Virgo, try to not be so nitpicking. You have a tendency to count everything, literally, from the number of nights your partner stays out late to the amount of time they spend on the phone. Don't overdo your controlling thing, Virgo, or Aquarius will rebel. Give the Water Bearer the freedom they need and this relationship may endure.

Virgo - Pisces

You are both sensitive by nature. You like to manage life in an organized way and be very clear about the things you do. You both enjoy other people and, in the end, your life goals are pretty similar, even though you set about achieving them in very different ways. There is potential for a good balance in your relationship and your relationship is an example of opposites on the zodiac wheel attracting. One of you tends to give and judge and give and judge. The other just gives and gives. One of you (Virgo) likes to diarize everything and expects the other to fit in. Pisces, you need independence and because of this, you need to let Virgo know that you intend to keep making your own arrangements, rather than hand over your diary to your Virgin. If you respect these differences this will be a strong relationship.

Libra

September 24 – October 23

Libra, you are often known for your great thinking ability and your communication skills. Your mind seems to be always working; seeking new ideas, exploring possibilities, and checking out the 'what ifs' in life.

Being mentally agile means you are usually able to get to the heart of issues easily and quickly. In fact, you are prone to making snap decisions.

Remember, the whole truth, the total situation, every aspect of a person is rarely revealed right away. So, try to resist the temptation to jump to conclusions at the outset of any situation. Take a breath and wait a moment.

Librans tend to express their feelings readily and are good at empathizing with others and, while they are known for their thinking abilities, it is rare for their hearts to take a back seat to their minds.

This is the astrological sign that represents marriage but you would be foolish to necessarily expect your Libran partner to be monogamous. Sure, they are into relationships. They love being involved; they love relationships so much that they tend to have lots of them, in fact. So, if you team up with a Libran, be prepared for your partner to have an interesting past – and honestly, isn't that what you love about them anyway?

Librans often present themselves in new situations with a flourish. Typically, they have a fairly unique and personable style. A Libran is generally well groomed, and seldom adopts a fashion just because it is IN. On the contrary, Librans enjoy developing their own style and, without doubt, it will reflect their character, personality and personal take on life.

Libra, you are ruled by the planet Venus and thus love is very much at the heart of this sign's makeup. Indeed, their goals in life often revolve around finding someone special, even if they don't intend to stay with them forever.

Libra Compatibility

Libra - Aries

Those born under the sign of Libra tend to very passionate and romantic and these qualities appeal to the Ram. At first, the attraction between you two may seem overwhelming but be warned, the love you share is likely to burn out almost as quickly as it started. You are opposites on the zodiac wheel and, in this instance, while you both are very attracted to each other, your relationship will only work if and when the Ram agrees to stop the chase and settle down.

Libra - Taurus

Libra, you are quite the romantic and your passionate nature is very attracted to the practical Bull. The Libran gives 100% to each and every relationship they have and this approach suits the hedonistic, sensual Taurus. Libra, remember your symbol is the Scales and, when it comes to matters of the heart, you need to aware that you can be easily thrown off balance. So, take care and don't run off at the first chance with someone new, leaving your Bull wondering what went wrong. While it may be in your nature to do so, it is up to you whether you choose to or not.

Libra - Gemini

This is a good match. You are both air signs and should be highly compatible. Both of you enjoy intellectual pursuits and, together, you should also enjoy a good social life. However, your styles of socializing and partying are quite different and your approaches may cause some friction between you. Libra, at parties you tend to hold back and attract people who interest you. On the other hand, your partner, Gemini will happily cruise off into the middle of the crowd and start chatting away. A word of advice! Gemini, try and slow down a bit and listen to your Libran partner and you will have a match that lasts as long as you both want.

Libra - Cancer

Libra, you are a romantic and your charms will seduce your Cancer, at least in the beginning. The Crab has a very nurturing nature and so, when you two meet, you will probably both feel like you have met your twin. It's almost as though you've finally found someone who understands the real you. Cancer, you need to relax and enjoy your relationship with Libra. Sure, this partnership may seem too good to be true but it doesn't have to be so. Together, you can live the dream.

Libra - Leo

Libra, you are a social animal and this is a very attractive quality to your Lion. While you both enjoy climbing the social ladder neither of you is crass enough to mention it outright. Your romantic relationship may start out as a friendship and, if so, this will form the cornerstone of your ongoing partnership. You are highly compatible. You are both romantics; you are both keen and willing to open up fully to your partner. Together, Leo and Libra could build a relationship that lasts a lifetime.

Libra - Virgo

Upfront, let's be honest. Being born under the sign of Virgo can mean being born with the potential to be tactless. So, in your relationship with Libra, guess who is likely to be the critical one? Guess who calls a spade a spade? Virgo, your frankness is too much for your more sensitive partner, Libra. So, if this relationship is to last, you need to take care what you say to Libra and how you say it. Libra, you are outwardly romantic and love little gestures of affection. Unfortunately, your partner will not be familiar with this way of expressing love and, if you want these romantic signs of affection, you're going to have to teach Virgo. Typically, the Virgin prefers to show their affection by doing things for you, rather than telling you. Can you live with this, Libra? Alternatively, can you learn a new way of expressing love, Virgo?

Libra - Libra

There seems to be a natural fit when Libra meets Libra. You are both considerate and understanding. You enjoy each other's company and yet, unusually for your star sign, you seem to know when to give your partner space. You probably feel quite secure in this relationship, and why not? Intuitively, one knows what the other needs and your enjoyment of similar interests means when you're together there's so much to talk about. Yours is a relationship that may well last.

Libra - Scorpio

Libra, you tend to seek out and enjoy the lighter moments in life and so, when you invite Scorpio into your life, you may be wondering what you've done. You see, there is often a darker side to Scorpio and, if this shows itself as jealousy, the Scales will have nothing to do with it. So, remember to keep your emotions in check, Scorpio. Libra, when Scorpio expresses the desire for personal space, don't think this is necessarily a poor reflection on you and your relationship. It could be, but don't jump to these conclusions immediately. Libra, you are the master of balance and your skill in maintaining a fine equilibrium will probably be tested by Scorpio. Nonetheless, your relationship has solid potential.

Libra - Sagittarius

You are attracted to each other but on the surface this attraction probably seems superficial to others. There is enough here to build a relationship on, but whether it will sustain you both is a different matter. You are both good communicators and sensitive to each other's needs. Sagittarius, remember your partner has an innate need to connect, not only with you but with others too. Respect that and give them the space they need. Libra, learn to deal with your partner's apparent flightiness and you two could go far together.

Libra - Capricorn

What happens when two natural born leaders meet and decide to form a love relationship? Sure, you could say that each of you leads in a different way but, essentially, it is in both your natures to rule. So, how do you handle this dilemma? Can you two make a go of this relationship? Of course you can and, when you do, you may just be the next power couple in your circle. While you both enjoy the finer things in life, the Goat tends to be more intent on marrying and settling down. So, is that what you want Libra? If it is, put some effort into getting Capricorn to loosen up a bit and you two will enjoy a strong, lasting bond.

Libra - Aquarius

You are both air signs and this means you enjoy intellectual pursuits. This is a good basis for your relationship. You enjoy each other's company but, should you decide to commit, be aware that your partnership could be lacking in passion. If that doesn't bother you, go for it. If it does, don't worry, you will always have a friend for life.

Libra - Pisces

Did you enjoy meeting each other? Did it feel like you'd finally met someone who had similar values to you? You see, you are both kind and thoughtful and you do value each other. While the Fish can be judgmental, on the upside, Libra, your partner is able to see things from most angles, including yours. This is a quality you will admire given it's one you probably don't possess. Are you looking for a formal arrangement with your Fish, Libra? If you are, you may have to wait because Pisces is oftentimes reluctant to commit too early.

Scorpio

October 24 - November 22

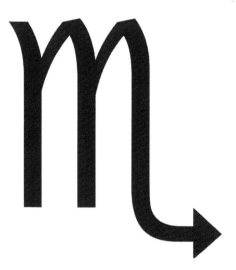

The powerful combination of mesmerizing eyes, a cool, reserved demeanor, a confident walk that falls just short of a swagger, and a commanding presence will naturally draws all eyes to Scorpio.

The physical appearance of a Scorpio can be very striking and they are also capable of exhibiting a quiet strength and gentle grace. Those born under the sign of Scorpio seem to be attractive to others on both a platonic and relationship level. In marked contrast to this image of the typical Scorpion is the seemingly contradictory ability that many of you have to come across as being uncaring.

This latter perception is only a façade. The truth is that Scorpio doesn't like sharing their deep feelings. However, anyone who wins the love of the Scorpion will know what it is to experience true love, affection and romance.

While the Scorpion may appear immune to stimulus around them, Scorpios are, in fact, very driven by pleasure and influenced by their surroundings. They seek the best in life and often consume it with an almost unbridled appetite – even if that leads them into some very dark recesses.

Scorpio, you need to guard against your innate tendency to embrace excess. Instead, focus on your goals and, once you do this, there is little that can come between you and your achievement of them. Coming second is not an option for Scorpio.

Giving up is also something that is foreign to the Scorpion, especially in conflict situations. Those born under the sign of Scorpio will battle long, fight smart, and persevere with ruthless determination. They don't take defeat well and will often retaliate with revenge, if the opportunity arises. So be on your guard, if you are planning to team up with a Scorpion.

Scorpio Compatibility

Scorpio - Aries

Aries, you are generally very independent and when you attract a Scorpio you have invited someone who is intense, emotional and possessive into your life. So, how is this going to work? You are both naturally controlling by nature and your relationship will only stay the distance if and when you both manage to rein in the jealous side of your natures. This partnership can work; it just needs quite a bit of work on both your parts.

Scorpio - Taurus

Can the Bull withstand the sting of the Scorpion? If anyone can, yes, a Taurean can. By nature, Scorpio is dominating, even possessive and while at first the Bull is able to withstand the sheer intensity of the Scorpion's focus, eventually they will be worn down by it and leave the relationship. That is not necessarily a bad thing for Taurus because the Bull does like its own company. So, Scorpio, do you feel confident enough in yourself and your relationship with your Bull to let them have their personal space? If you don't, you will lose them.

Scorpio - Gemini

What an unusual pairing. It's as though you two are from different planets. Have you ever really got to know anyone like your partner before? The essence of who and what you are is so truly foreign to each of you. Therein lies the mystery, the intrigue, the allure and the attraction. Add to this, the sociability of Gemini and the passionate nature of Scorpio and this becomes an intriguing mix. Will your relationship last? Stranger things have happened than will come out of this pairing but you may be wise to enjoy each other in the moment and take each day as it comes.

Scorpio - Cancer

Scorpio has a tendency to be jealous. Can you deal with this side of your partner, Cancer? Or is it too much like looking into the mirror? It could very well feel like this because you are both familiar with the ugly side of jealousy. Sure, there are differences in where your jealousy springs from – for one it is ego driven and, for the other, oftentimes your jealousy stems from your own personal insecurity. There is a trick to avoiding claws and fangs and clashing of heads and that is to mark out your own territory, within your relationship. You are compatible. You just need to learn how to live together.

Scorpio - Leo

A common and strong link between you two is your determination. Chances are, in the beginning of your relationship, you will both show off your passionate sides. Later on, however, this burning passion you both feel could turn into hot clashes; that is, unless Scorpio agrees to be the power behind Leo's throne. Your relationship is ruled by domination and this is not necessarily an easy route for either of you to travel. Try being kinder to each other. Be gentle on yourselves and your relationship. That way, you may enjoy your partnership, rather than just endure it.

Scorpio - Virgo

People born under these signs tend to be very practical and this can get very annoying. Virgo, do you nag your Scorpion? You don't need to, you know. They know what's expected of them but the Virgin just can't help themselves. Try and relax around each other more. You are a good match. When you, Scorpio, become quiet, it could mean you're going into one of your moods. It could also mean you want time to yourself. Virgo, learn to read your partner's moods and respect their need for solitude. There is always plenty for you to do to keep yourself busy.

Scorpio - Libra

Libra, you tend to seek out and enjoy the lighter moments in life and so, when you invite Scorpio into your life, you may be wondering what you've done. You see, there is often a darker side to Scorpio and, if this shows itself as jealousy, the Scales will have nothing to do with it. So, remember to keep your emotions in check, Scorpio. Libra, when Scorpio expresses the desire for personal space, do not think this is necessarily a poor reflection on you and your relationship. It could be, but don't jump to these conclusions immediately. Libra, you are the master of balance and your skill in maintaining a fine equilibrium will probably be tested by Scorpio. Nonetheless, your relationship has solid potential.

Scorpio - Scorpio

Pairing a Scorpio with another Scorpio is like topping up fire with fire. You both need to be in control so how ever are you going to work this relationship out? Do you even really want to try? If you two manage not to clash at the outset of your relationship then it will be worth your while to try and work things out using your passion. You are both very passionate by nature and this may be the key you need to unlock the potential of your relationship. You are equals; acknowledge this and see how far you can go together.

Scorpio - Sagittarius

If this relationship is to even get off the ground, you two will have to put in a lot of effort. This is not a natural partnership. Sure, you both like exploring but, Sagittarius, your wanderlust takes you into the far corners of the world while your partner prefers to explore the far reaches of their inner psyche. Furthermore, the Archer seems to have a lighter energy than the Scorpion and, if the latter doesn't manage to lighten up a little, Sagittarius will probably be repelled by the dark side of their Scorpion and leave the relationship. On the upside, Sagittarius, you have an innate ability to turn relationships into friendships and so, even if you two don't last as a couple, you will probably both end up with a lifelong friend.

Scorpio - Capricorn

These two signs have one huge trait in common. Can you guess what it is? You are both highly ambitious. Of course, you show your ambition to the world in very different ways. Capricorn, while you are more outwardly ambitious than your partner, there is nothing brash or showy in the way you present to the world. Scorpio, you are more restrained when it comes to showing off your drive. As a couple, you should seek out ways to support each another, rather than compete against one another. You need to remember that because ambition drives you personally and professionally and consumes a lot of your energy and attention, there may not be much passion in your relationship or indeed, opportunities to show affection openly. It is unlikely that this will bother either of you, though.

Scorpio - Aquarius

This is not an easy match. Potentially, you two could start a war for two between yourselves. Are you up for this? Are you prepared to risk this happening? If you want to give this relationship a go then, the Water Bearer must understand that you, Scorpio, do not necessarily agree with the way they express their values. Aquarius, while you may be out to save the world and stand up publicly to do so, this is not necessarily Scorpio's idea of nirvana. The Scorpion prefers a more private life, one where, while they may harbor similar values to yours, Aquarius, they will not seek to publicly declare them. How badly do you want each other? How much are you two prepared to compromise? The outcome of your relationship depends on your responses.

Scorpio - Pisces

This is a good match. You are both empathetic and naturally aware of the other's needs. You are both passionate and Scorpio, if you can trust your Fish more and be less suspicious of them, you will find the Fish a faithful partner. Pisces, you need to let Scorpio know, in no uncertain terms, that you hate being scrutinized. Pisces needs their freedom and Scorpio, you need to put away your microscope and trust your partner more. For your part, Pisces, you need to play down the secrecy thing and not overplay your intuition. If you don't, you are likely to drive Scorpio mad.

Sagittarius

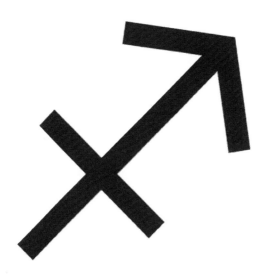

November 23 – December 21

You, Sagittarius, are optimistic, frank, adventurous, endearing and a paradox. You are full of contradictions.

On the outside, you appear to be affable and fun loving. Yet, there's a depth of emotion rarely seen in others. In dealing with a Sagittarian, what needs to be remembered is that the Centaur is half man, half beast, and the latter part often dominates. While a Sagittarian tends to be candid, there's also a part of them that could be described as being more devious than Pisces, more deceptive than Gemini and more carnal than Scorpio.

Don't be deceived by the fact that your Sagittarian looks like they're breezing through life. They aren't actually. A true Sagittarian will seek out truth, understanding, meaning and purpose in all that they do and this depth of enquiry should not be overlooked.

Sagittarians are generally very in tune with the moment. They like to move into the flow and stay there for as long as possible. On the one hand, they act on instinct and intuition and yet, on the other, they can be goal oriented and very focused on the end game. It is often the case that the Centaur has an agenda and where possible, they will take advantage of opportunities as they arise.

At heart, a true Sagittarian is a gambler, willing to risk all to win all. The Centaur also values its freedom highly. This too can impinge on their ability to form and maintain lasting relationships.

Sagittarius Compatibility

Sagittarius - Aries

People born under these two signs should get along well. You are both enthusiastic, optimistic and have positive outlooks on life. Furthermore, Aries, you are more likely than most signs to overlook your Archer's controlling ways. But have you noticed their tactlessness? Aries, while you come across as very strong willed and determined, and indeed you are these things, you need to remind Sagittarius that your strength does not make you immune to hurt. Is the Archer too critical of your appearance? Does the Archer put down your achievements? If they do, you have a few options: toughen up, don't let Sagittarius get to you, insist that the Archer aim their insults elsewhere, or leave. Your choice! Just don't let the Archer walk over you.

Sagittarius - Taurus

The key word to this relationship is faithfulness. Taurus, do you fully understand that when Sagittarius pledges their undying love and devotion to you they really do mean it – in their own way? Throughout their lives, Sagittarians tend to attract a lot of partners and this long relationship record has a tendency to upset the much more faithful Taurus. So, at the first sign that Sagittarius is back playing the love field, Taurus, you would be well advised to take your leave and move on.

Sagittarius - Gemini

You are both free spirits. You dislike being pinned down too much, are happiest when exploring life and you both welcome change and challenges. You are also both risk takers and so, one or both of you needs to be more careful than your nature would suggest. Unfortunately, there are not the usual checks and balances that usually arise in relationships and so, you are likely to push the limits too far in life, in your relationship and in all that you do together. Be aware of this to avoid unnecessary suffering. The Archer likes things straight up – no waffle, no frills, no embellishments – so Gemini, get to the point as soon and as often as you can when talking to your partner. Save your sweet lead-ins for others. Conversely, the Archer would do well to curb their bluntness and soften their words when speaking to the Twins.

Sagittarius - Cancer

Upfront, answer this question. Both of you! Why do you want to be together? Have you given much thought to what each of you brings to your relationship? Individually, both your star signs are great. However, when you two get together is when the clashes seem to start. Have you noticed that about your relationship yet? If you want to, and if it's not too late, why don't you consider ending this relationship and waiting for more suitable partners? If you are already committed to each other, then Cancer, you might like to try backing off and giving your Sagittarius space – loads of space. As you may have gathered by now, (or perhaps you haven't worked it out yet), your Centaur does not like to be hemmed in. And, Cancer, what can you do to help your relationship? Try curbing your need to smother your partner – truth be told, they don't like feeling stifled. These are big asks of both of you.

Sagittarius - Leo

What a happy couple this star sign combination makes! Your sunny dispositions and love of life and fun shine through for the world to see. One sticking point in your relationship could be the matter of freedom. Leo, have you noticed how you love to reign in your Sagittarius? This is not a particularly good thing to do if you want the Archer to stick around. Sagittarius, you love your freedom and there is no doubt about it, your Lion must allow you to roam freely. How else can it be? Leo, you are a very sensitive star sign and, if Sagittarius hurts you with their barbed comments you will quickly retreat from them to lick your wounds. Be aware of this, Sagittarius, and don't purposely set out to hurt your Lion's pride. You may just hurt Leo once too often.

Sagittarius - Virgo

Sagittarius, you like experimenting with different relationships and in Virgo, you will find an interesting partner. That is, if you get the chance to partner with the Virgin. You see Virgo is far more choosey than you are. They will let you know in no uncertain terms what they think about your long list of relationships, your seemingly tarty behavior, and your obvious need to explore different couplings. Your style is not Virgo's style! So, Virgo, while you may feel that the excitement you bring to your relationship with the Centaur is a valuable contribution don't be surprised if you are left feeling underappreciated in this partnership.

Sagittarius - Libra

You are attracted to each other but on the surface this attraction probably seems superficial to others. There is enough here to build a relationship on but whether it will sustain you both is a different matter. You are both good communicators and sensitive to each other's needs. Sagittarius, remember your partner has an innate need to connect, not only with you but with others too. Respect that and give them the space they need. Libra, learn to deal with your partner's apparent flightiness and you two could go far together.

Sagittarius - Scorpio

If this relationship is to even get off the ground, you two will have to put in a lot of effort. This is not a natural partnership. Sure, you both like exploring but Sagittarius your wanderlust takes you into the far corners of the world while your partner prefers to explore the far reaches of their inner psyche. Furthermore, the Archer seems to have a lighter energy than the Scorpion and, if the latter doesn't manage to lighten up a little, Sagittarius will probably be repelled by the dark side of their Scorpion and leave the relationship. On the upside, Sagittarius, you have an innate ability to turn relationships into friendships and so, even if you two don't last as a couple, you will probably both end up with a lifelong friend.

Sagittarius - Sagittarius

This pairing has loads of potential and few downsides. Being Sagittarians, you are both big thinkers. You like to aim for the stars and often you do hit the moon. However, let's be a bit practical for a moment. Which of you is going to be the practical partner in this relationship? Money? Where is it come from? What about holidays? Who will arrange these? Where will you live? Which of you is more inclined to attend to the mundane things in life? Neither of you is naturally practical and for this relationship to work, you are going to have to help each other out. If you can do this and, it's likely you will, you'll have a great life together. Enjoy your adventures and enjoy each other!

Sagittarius - Capricorn

How are you two going? You are very different to each other but, then again, you knew that before you started your relationship. Everyone did! Typically, Capricorn likes to hold back, weigh things up, assess all the options before committing to a partner and, where you're concerned Sagittarius, the Goat will think even longer and harder before committing. This is because they're well aware of the magnitude of differences between you. However, your opposite natures can be attractive. Capricorn, you are more cautious than your sunny-sided Sagittarius and this, together with your tendency to be realistic, could eventually weigh too heavily on your partner. Needed most in this relationship are compromises and an ongoing willingness to meet the challenges that will inevitably arise because of the fundamental differences in your natures.

Sagittarius - Aquarius

You are very compatible, but then you probably know that already. You are both laidback in your approach to life and independent too. If your relationship does come to an end, it will likely be that it fizzles out rather than explodes. If this does happen and you go your separate ways where love is concerned, you will probably be friends for life. At the beginning of your relationship, just pay attention to the romance and, chances are, you won't be greeting each other as friends, rather than lovers, anytime soon.

Sagittarius - Pisces

While you are both flexible and can adjust to each other's needs, the main differences between you lie in the way you think and how you approach things. Quick as a flash, Sagittarius, you like to make decisions. Sometimes you even forget to consider your Piscean partner's feelings. On the other hand, the Fish is more intuitive and likes to soak up the mood, absorb the vibe slowly and ultimately show their sensitive side. So you, the Archer, needs to be careful where and how you shoot off your verbal arrows. If they hit your Fish you will wound them deeply and, before you even notice, Pisces will withdraw, hurt. You two could make a go of this relationship but that depends on how much effort you are prepared to put in.

Capricorn

December 22 – January 20

Your sign is tied to the earth and this affects the choices you make and the goals you set. Ever practical, linear, detailed, and steadfastly focused, you, the Goat, need to guard against becoming too anal.

The Capricorn loves to work, loves to accomplish things and your greatest efforts are always aimed at a higher goal. Working for the sake of working doesn't appeal to the Capricorn mentality. Working for a higher purpose does.

As a Capricorn, you are dependable and honest and you can be relied upon to keep any promises made. Capricorns are certainly capable of saying no. You just say no in a polite, indirect way that rarely causes offence. Typically, the Capricorn is very thoughtful, able to inject tremendous vision into projects, and add hope and imagination into their life plans and goals.

The methodical nature of the Capricorn's work ethic may fool some into minimizing the Capricorn's intellect. To do so is to make a mistake. Capricorns can have razor sharp intellects, so proceed with caution, watch your Capricorn in action, and be amazed.

Establishing and maintaining relationships can be difficult for some Capricorns. You tend to be solitary, self-reliant individuals, focused on the task at hand with little time for the frivolous social banter that's required to start a friendship or ignite a romance. Given time, however, lots of time, Capricorn will open up about their feelings. Your partner needs to be made aware of just how long this can take and of course, be prepared to wait and be patient.

By nature, Capricorns are thrifty and they enjoy getting the most value out of each and every one of life's resources. This includes money, time, energy and relationships. Above all else, the Capricorn yearns for and admires substance, reliability and proven performance.

Capricorn Compatibility

Capricorn - Aries

While you respect each other's individual qualities you both have quite different approaches to life. You both love success but Aries, you prefer to skip light-heartedly through life, while your friend, the Goat, is more serious and conservative. Chances are that Aries will attempt to lighten up this relationship with Capricorn at some stage but it needs to be remembered this can only be done if the Goat agrees. You see, Capricorn is likely to dig in their heels if anyone, even their partner, tries to move them in a direction they don't want to go in. Aries, if you are patient with your Capricorn, you will enjoy a remarkable relationship.

Capricorn - Taurus

Taurus and Capricorn are both practical types of people, and devoted lovers. However, the tenderness that you share in your relationship will depart, even if the Goat doesn't, if Capricorn feels taken for granted in any way. So, if there's the possibility that either of you is not looking for a long-term, monogamous relationship, then you will both be better off looking elsewhere for what you need. You are both earth signs but that bond is not enough to necessarily bind you together indefinitely.

Capricorn - Gemini

These star signs are opposites. Gemini, you are the outgoing member of this partnership. You love people and socializing and being involved and, Capricorn, you are far more reserved than your partner. So, the question for you is this: can you both accept your obvious differences and not be tempted to change each other too much? If you can, there will be longevity in your relationship. If you can't resist the temptation to change your partner your relationship will be short lived.

Capricorn - Cancer

You are both deeply attracted to each other and share a mutual love of stability. This is a great start for your relationship. However, because you are both very predictable, even conservative, things may get a bit boring even for you. To avoid this, all that really needs to happen is for the Goat to open up more and share their feelings with their partner. Get the communication right, avoid the rut and you two could be on the road to a lasting relationship, one that is based on friendship, companionship, loyalty and balance.

Capricorn - Leo

Capricorn, you are more reserved and less open to expressing your feelings than your partner, Leo. This difference will probably be the primary source of discord in your relationship. You two are certainly good where business matters are concerned but when it comes to the romantic side of your relationship, you will have to work extra hard to make it work. Capricorn, you need to learn to be more open with your feelings and show affection for your Lion in public more. Similarly, the Lion partner needs to allow the Goat to get on with their work. You are both intrinsically loyal and, if you find a good balance, your relationship will flourish. Look for that compromise position and you will enjoy a happy relationship.

Capricorn - Virgo

You are both practical earth signs and, while this down-to-earth quality might seem boring to some, to you it is the stuff of which your love is made. You are very compatible. Yours is a match made in the stars. So, enjoy each other and don't worry what the outside world may think of you and your mutual love of financial planning, etc. You are a good match for each other.

Capricorn - Libra

What happens when two natural born leaders meet and decide to form a love relationship? Sure, you could say that each of you leads in a different way but, essentially, it is in both your natures to rule. So, how do you handle this dilemma? Can you two make a go of this relationship? Of course you can and, when you do, you may just be the next power couple in your circle. While you both enjoy the finer things in life, the Goat tends to be more intent on marrying and settling down. So, is that what you want Libra? If it is, put some effort into getting Capricorn to loosen up a bit and you two will enjoy a strong, lasting bond.

Capricorn - Scorpio

These two signs have one huge trait in common. Can you guess what it is? You are both highly ambitious. Of course, you show your ambition to the world in very different ways. Capricorn, while you are more outwardly ambitious than your partner there is nothing brash or showy in the way you present to the world. Scorpio, you are more restrained when it comes to showing off your drive. As a couple, you should seek out ways to support each another, rather than compete against one another. You need to remember that because ambition drives you personally and professionally and consumes a lot of your energy and attention, there may not be much passion in your relationship or indeed, opportunities to show affection openly. It is unlikely that this will bother either of you, though.

Capricorn - Sagittarius

How are you two going? You are very different to each other but, then again, you knew that before you started your relationship. Everyone did! Typically, Capricorn likes to hold back, weigh things up, assess all the options before committing to a partner and, where you're concerned, Sagittarius, the Goat will think even longer and harder before committing. This is because they're well aware of the magnitude of differences between you. However, your opposite natures can be attractive. Capricorn, you are more cautious than your sunny-sided Sagittarius and this, together with your tendency to be realistic, could eventually weigh too heavily on your partner. Needed most in this relationship are numerous compromises and an ongoing willingness to meet the challenges that will inevitably arise because of the fundamental differences in your natures.

Capricorn - Capricorn

This is the best of all pairings for the Capricorn. Capricorns really do get along well with other Capricorns. Being the Goat means enjoying the company of those who have the same worldview as you do and seeking out a partner who is willing to work steadfastly towards the same goals as you. Who better to do this with than another Capricorn? Essentially, the Goat is honest, reliable, frugal and diligent and these are the very traits they are attracted to in their Capricorn partner.

Capricorn - Aquarius

Capricorn, do you like unpredictability and spontaneity? Truthfully, do you? Didn't think so. So, why are you teamed up with Aquarius? The Water Bearer rejects the status quo. Aquarius loves change, even for change's sake. There's little your partner likes better than being whimsical and yet here you two are trying to make a go of it. You do share some common ground; namely, the desire to set and achieve goals. Your best chance for success will occur when Aquarius stops behaving outrageously, just to provoke a response from the Goat, and Capricorn loosens up a bit.

Capricorn - Pisces

Pisces, you are the dreamer and who better to help you ground your dreams than your Goat? Capricorn, you are so intent on matter and form and how things look and should be, whatever can your dreamy Fish offer you? Magic! Pure and simple magic! Pisces brings little bits of lightness, even flair and creativity, to your relationship. The Goat tends to be industrious and hard working and could, if Pisces is so inclined, form the bedrock on which the Fish builds their dream. So, Capricorn, you need to appreciate your charming Pisces more, just like others do, and Pisces, continue to weave your magic and don't let Capricorn ground you down. If you do, you will have a partnership that complements your personal natures and is likely to last.

Aquarius

January 21 – February 19

You are fortunate to be an Aquarius because you are known as the humanitarian zodiac sign. You are progressive in your thinking, which is reflected in every aspect of your life. You do not like being told how to live your life, and you will make your decisions clear to anyone who dares question them.

You are energetic, with a zest for life. Unfortunately, society's boundaries can still be insurmountable, even for an Aquarian such as yourself. You are very much in charge of your own destiny and, if something or someone gets in the way of your aspirations, you won't give up on your goals easily. This perseverance earns you respect from others, even if they disagree with what you are hoping to accomplish.

You have great organizational and communicative skills and, for this reason, you work well when teamed with others who have similar aspirations. You enjoy sharing your unique take on life and you often suggest interesting solutions to problems that come your way. You always try to stay true to yourself and, even if other people challenge your unconventional thoughts and beliefs, you will happily prove these naysayers wrong.

As far as relationships are concerned, you have difficulty keeping them on an even keel. This is due to your innate need for constant change. You will find happiness, both in friendship and in love, if you seek out those who keep up with your craving for 'new', have a social conscience and are able to evolve with you.

As an Aquarian, the great thing about you is your ability to accept your partner for who they are and not restrict them in any way. Your energetic and passionate nature draws people to you. When you are in a relationship, you have no trouble changing things that are detrimental to it or you. This makes it easier for you to maintain a lasting partnership – just make sure it is with the right person.

Aquarius Compatibility

Aquarius - Aries

The Aries partner will usually take the initiative in this relationship and the Water Bearer will not keep you from doing as you please. Aries, you are adventurous and decisive, even courageous, and these qualities are much admired by your Aquarius. Be aware, however, of the issue of privacy in your relationship, as you may have different ideas about what this word means.

Aquarius - Taurus

This is a match that can go either way. Ask yourselves this! Is there something about the other that seems to inexplicably draw you to them, even though on the surface you are so different? You probably realize by now that your relationship requires an enormous amount of work, compromise, and understanding. That's a big ask for anyone! However, given the innate determination that you both share, you may just be able to add this relationship to your personal lists of achievements.

Aquarius - Gemini

You are both air signs and that's a good thing. Both of you love freedom and are happy not weaving a web to entrap your partner. This, too, is a good sign. So, where is the catch? Have you noticed the lack of depth in your relationship yet? The Water Bearer loves tackling a cause – ecology, the environment, education, equality – and Aquarius, while your partner may start off as enthusiastically as you do, ultimately Gemini is likely to lose focus. Knowing this fundamental difference gives you a chance to adjust your expectations of your relationship. You can make a good go of this and, romantically, you are very compatible.

Aquarius - Cancer

Cancer, you and your Aquarian partner are both friendly and intense. Aquarius, you would do well to learn to be more compassionate with your Crab. Cancer, try not to run, at least in the beginning, from the conservative lifestyle that you two will no doubt build together. If you do feel the need to flee, chances are you will ruin your relationship because you will likely find comfort and excitement in the arms of another. It is unlikely this relationship will last a lifetime but you may as well enjoy each other for a while at least.

Aquarius - Leo

Mmm! This is a bit of a strange coupling. Aquarius, you need to try and be more personable when Leo is around. Otherwise, you'll find that you've kept the personal entourage of friends that surrounds you and you will have lost Leo. The Water Bearer likes freedom so don't try and cramp their style. At heart, Aquarians are freedom-loving creatures who strongly resist any attempts to hem them in. So, Leo, even though you love to rule, if you impose your authority over Aquarius, they will simply turn and leave you.

Aquarius - Virgo

The bond between Virgo and Aquarius is more intellectual than emotional. This is an unusual coupling to say the least. For your relationship to have a chance of success, the Virgin need to lighten up and the Water Bearer needs to resist the temptation to rebel, just because they can. Virgo, try and not be so nitpicking. You have a tendency to count everything, literally, from the number of nights your partner stays out late to the amount of time they spend on the phone. Don't overdo your controlling thing, Virgo, or Aquarius will rebel. Give the Water Bearer the freedom they need and this relationship may endure.

Aquarius - Libra

You are both air signs and this means you both enjoy intellectual pursuits. This is a good basis for a relationship. You certainly enjoy each other's company and, should you decide to commit to a long-term relationship, be aware that your partnership will probably be lacking in passion. If this doesn't bother you and you feel you can always work on this area of your love life later, then go for it. If it does bother you, don't worry, you two will always be there for each other as friends.

Aquarius - Scorpio

This is not an easy match. Potentially, you two could start a war for two between yourselves. Are you up for this? Are you prepared to risk this happening? If you want to give this relationship a go then, the Water Bearer must understand that you, Scorpio, do not necessarily agree with the way they express their values. Aquarius, while you may be out to save the world and stand up publicly to do so, this is not necessarily Scorpio's idea of nirvana. The Scorpion prefers a more private life, one where, while they may harbor similar values to yours, Aquarius, they will not seek to publicly declare them. How badly do you want each other? How much are you two prepared to compromise? The outcome of your relationship depends on your responses.

Aquarius - Sagittarius

You are very compatible but then you probably know that already. You are both laidback in your approach to life, and independent too. If your relationship does come to an end, it will likely be that it fizzles out rather than explodes. If this does happen and you go your separate ways where love is concerned, you will probably be friends for life. At the beginning of your relationship, just pay attention to the romance and, chances are, you won't be greeting each other as friends, rather than lovers, anytime soon.

Aquarius - Capricorn

Capricorn, do you like unpredictability and spontaneity? Truthfully, do you? Didn't think so. So, why are you teamed up with Aquarius? The Water Bearer rejects the status quo. Aquarius loves change, even for change's sake. There's little your partner likes better than being whimsical and yet, here you two are trying to make a go of it. You do share some common ground; namely, the desire to set and achieve goals. Your best chance for success will occur when Aquarius stops behaving outrageously, just to provoke a response from the Goat, and Capricorn loosens up a bit.

Aquarius - Aquarius

Two Aquarians in a love match will work. However, because of the doubling of the force of your nature, you are like two tornadoes sweeping through life. Your force is doubly strong; your challenge is to use it as a force for good, not destruction. Make the most of your fun-loving natures but be careful not to let the frivolity take over. Between the two of you, you are able to do many things. It's just a matter of which direction you decide upon, together, and where you ultimately decide to direct your energies.

Aquarius - Pisces

There are similarities between your signs and once your friends start to see the rhythm that develops in your relationship they will understand why you two get along so well. You both love freedom and enjoy your time together, and your time apart. Pisces, you're the dreamer in this partnership. You rely on your intuition more than anything else so don't play with your Water Bearer's emotions by using what appears to others to be your ability to gather secrets as a weapon against your partner. Aquarius, don't try and impose your logical way of thinking and doing on your Fish. If you two can sort out these differences, your relationship stands a chance of enduring.

Pisces

February 20 – March 19

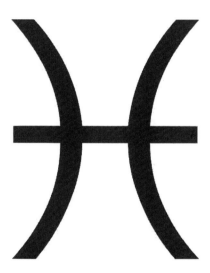

Pisces is the last sign of the Zodiac and the most spiritually mature. Being a Piscean means being compassionate and able to love unconditionally. You are empathetic, genuinely care about your fellow man and will usually go out of your way to help someone in need. Your friends can count on you to be a shoulder to cry on. However, beware, as some Pisceans like to tell it like it is.

One of the areas in life where Pisces struggles is making hard decisions. Pisces can see most situations from most angles and this is what makes it hard for them to decide. It's as though they have information overload and it is no wonder, because Pisces are the most intuitive of all the signs.

You are fond of culture, music and art and love being surrounded with classic finery. You want the world to be perfect, but it isn't, Pisces. You are an idealist and a dreamer, and part of your challenge is to accept what can't be changed in life.

Pisces, you are free-spirited, independent, mysterious and malleable, meaning you adapt and change, depending on the circumstances and the person you are with.

Pisces Compatibility

Pisces - Aries

Pisces is great at providing emotional support, and throwing people off track. The first quality is appealing but the latter is infuriating for an Aries. On the surface, the Pisces appears easy to dominate. This may be the case in the beginning of the relationship but, the more Aries dominates, the more the Fish will feel the need to escape. There is hope for this relationship as long as you can find a balance between domination and submission.

Pisces - Taurus

Pisces, you are everyone's soul mate, or so it seems, even the Bull's. Give each other space and 'me' time and you will get along well. Taurus, you are known for your perseverance and this personal quality is enough to at least get Pisces' attention. Taurus, you will keep the interest of your Pisces partner if you are prepared to receive all that the bountiful and nurturing Pisces has to give.

Pisces - Gemini

These two star signs are generally up for trying anything new and, within this pairing, there is much to explore. Both Pisces and Gemini enjoy their own personal freedom and, indeed, are happy to accommodate this quality in their partnership. Gemini, while you are attracted to Pisces' sensitivity and wisdom, to ensure your relationship lasts, you need to hone your intuition a bit more, so that you can develop a deeper understanding of your Piscean partner.

Pisces - Cancer

Cancer, you and Pisces are similar natured. You both tend to be emotional and are sympathetic and compassionate. However, for this relationship to last, you both need to let down your guards. The Fish will embrace the Crab. In return, the Crab needs to be wary of not overwhelming the Fish. If you both really work at your relationship it will work, but if either of you is unwilling to really compromise, it is probably best that you move on. Cancer, you hate lying and Pisces, while you are not prone to outright lying, your exaggerations will get to your Crab partner. If both of you are willing to work at this partnership it will happen, if only for as long as you can sustain the effort.

Pisces - Leo

Pisces is usually out to shower the one they love with love and loads of affection and attention. This suits Leo just fine. To an outsider, this relationship looks like one in which the Lion rules and the Fish is happy to be submissive. However, things are not always what they seem when Pisces is involved. Pisces, you are more secretive than your Lion partner and Leo, you love to put all of you out there on display for others to see and admire. For this relationship to last you will have to indulge and accommodate the marked difference you have. Are you up to the challenge?

Pisces - Virgo

You are both sensitive by nature. You like to manage life in an organized way and be very clear about the things you do. You both enjoy other people and, in the end, your life goals are pretty similar, even though you set about achieving them in very different ways. There is potential for a good balance in your relationship and your relationship is an example of opposites on the zodiac wheel attracting. One of you tends to give and judge and give and judge. The other just gives and gives. One of you (Virgo) likes to diarize everything and expects the other to fit in. Pisces, you need independence and because of this, you need to let Virgo know that you intend to keep making your own arrangements, rather than hand over your diary to your Virgin. If you respect these differences this will be a strong relationship.

Pisces - Libra

Did you enjoy the moment when you first met each other? Did it feel like you'd finally found someone who had similar values to you? Hope so! You see, you are both kind and thoughtful and you do value each other a lot. While the Fish is prone to being judgmental, on the upside, Libra, your partner is able to see things from most angles, and that includes your own. Libra, this is a quality you are sure to admire, given it's one that you probably don't possess. Are you looking to formalize this arrangement with your Fish, Libra? If you are, you may be moving too fast for Pisces. The Fish is oftentimes reluctant to commit too early, so be patient.

Pisces - Scorpio

This is a good match. You are both empathetic and naturally aware of the other's needs. You are both passionate and Scorpio, if you can trust your Fish more and be less suspicious of them, you will find the Fish a faithful partner. Pisces, you need to let Scorpio know, in no uncertain terms, that you hate being scrutinized. Pisces needs their freedom and Scorpio you need to put away your microscope and trust your partner more. For your part, Pisces, you need to play down the secrecy thing and not overplay your intuition. If you don't, you are likely to drive Scorpio mad.

Pisces - Sagittarius

While you are both flexible and can adjust to each other's needs, the main differences between you lie in the way you think and how you approach things. Quick as a flash, Sagittarius, you like to make decisions. Sometimes you even forget to consider your Piscean partner's feelings. On the other hand, the Fish is more intuitive and likes to soak up the mood, absorb the vibe slowly and ultimately show their sensitive side.

So you, the Archer, needs to be careful where and how you shoot off your verbal arrows. If they hit your Fish you will wound them deeply and, before you even notice, Pisces will withdraw, hurt. You two could make a go of this relationship but that depends on how much

Pisces - Capricorn

Pisces, you are the dreamer and who better to help you ground your dreams than your Goat? Capricorn, you are so intent on matter and form and how things look and should be, whatever can your dreamy Fish offer you? Magic! Pure and simple magic! Pisces brings little bits of lightness, even flair and creativity, to your relationship. The Goat tends to be industrious and hard working and could, if Pisces is so inclined, form the bedrock on which the Fish builds their dream. So, Capricorn, you need to appreciate your charming Pisces more, just like others do, and Pisces, continue to weave your magic and don't let Capricorn ground you down. If you do, you will have a partnership that complements your personal natures and is likely to last.

Pisces - Aquarius

There are similarities between your signs and once your friends start to see the rhythm that develops in your relationship they will understand why you two get along so well. You both love freedom and enjoy your time together, and your time apart. Pisces, you're the dreamer in this partnership. You rely on your intuition more than anything else so don't play with your Water Bearer's emotions by using what appears to others to be your ability to gather secrets as a weapon against your partner. Aquarius, don't try and impose your logical way of thinking and doing on your Fish. If you two can sort out these differences, your relationship stands a chance of enduring.

Pisces - Pisces

This partnership could go either way, and the way that it does go will change from moment to moment. Sure Pisces, you are the most intuitive of all the zodiac signs and, because of this, you can read each other very well. However, you are also highly mutable, meaning you both change according to your circumstances. So, if you happen to shift in different directions at the same time, you may find yourselves apart and out of sync. Then there is the issue of who will take the lead in the relationship, and when. Good communication skills are required in this partnership to ensure that your relationship moves forwards, rather than drifts in circles.

Thank You

Thank you for reading this book and trusting me to offer you some insights into astrology and its impact on relationships.

If you are interested in human nature and relationships then I suggest you subscribe to my website, **Compatibility and Love.** If you are more into the paranormal and the meaning of life then my **Psychic Revolution** is probably the blog that will interest you most.

Of course, I'd also love you to buy another of my books and share it with your friends but, even if you don't, I hope you'll at least check out my blogs.

Cheers

Rosemary

PS: If you enjoyed this book, please let others know. A great way to do this is to go now to **Amazon** click the 'Liked' button at the top of the page and leave a review.

Made in the USA
Lexington, KY
07 December 2012